How to Demand a Paycheck

"By What You Invest."

By Victor Jenkins

www.TennesseeSounds.com

Published by
The Grass House Publishing Co.
Kingsport, TN 37664
www.GrassHousePublishing.com

The Grass House Publishing Co.
1001 N. Eastman Rd STE C
Kingsport, TN 37664
www.GrassHousePublishing.com
Ordering Information:
Quantity sales. Special discounts are available on quantity purchases by corporations, associations, and others. For details, contact the publisher at the address above.

Editing, Cover, & Interior design by Alex Johnson

Printed in the United States of America

First Edition

Foreword

This book is a work of love from the author to you - the reader. While the probability of success is as variable as accurately predicting the weather, you have the power and opportunity to lead the life that you desire.

Alex Johnson, editor

How to Demand a Paycheck

How to Demand a Paycheck

My name is Victor Jenkins. I am the owner of Tennessee Sounds a music store in the Greenacres Shopping Plaza in Kingsport Tennessee. I've been in the music business approximately 35 years. Back in the late 70s I was at all music festivals for bluegrass that I could get to from the state of Michigan every weekend. I was not only there for business but I also met and became friends with many of the top bluegrass musicians in the country. I sold instruments and accessories and everything related to the bluegrass world, guitars, banjos, mandolins and violins. It gave me a chance to firsthand experience what it takes to become a professional musician. Most of the musicians I became acquainted with were back porch pickers or in house players that never planned on stepping on stage.

Regardless of how well you play or sing, others around you will always tell you what a good job you have done. Unfortunately this is not always the truth. Most musicians and singers do not really want to hear the truth. They would rather think they are better than what they really are.

How to Demand a Paycheck

I have decided to write this book in hopes of helping musicians build, grow, and maintain ambition in order to facilitate their success. Constructive criticism is the best kind but sometimes it is the hardest to swallow. I have taught music for over 30 years. Guitar and banjo have been my focus, but I emphasize growing your vocal talent while learning the songs I am teaching them to play. The one thing about bluegrass musicians, you must know the song in order to play it with feeling. If you are able to sing the song that you wish to play, the melody itself is the most important part of playing. Songs that do not have a melody do not make sense. If you play, Mary had a Little Lamb, over 90% of all people that hear this song will recognize it by the syllables that you have played. All melodies are spoken or played in syllables.

Music is played with two purposes in mind. One, to accompany the singer, to make him sound the best you possibly can, to set the tempo and the key that this song is sung in. The only other reason for playing music is to replace the singer and by replacing the singer you must play the melody in syllables. Music that is played by scales will never make sense because it is an arrangement of noise. Music is played on three levels, high, low, and midrange. Any arrangement of these sounds that do not pronounce the words of the song can never make sense. If you play any combination of sounds over and over it will be recognized, but never make sense. This is why musicians that strictly play instrumental have a more difficult time making it famous. An arrangement of noise may sound beautiful, but generally speaking it is not what people what to hear. People go to shows, concerts, and picking sessions for one reason, to hear the singer perform his songs. Singing adds a level of emotional connection the audience cannot obtain without hearing a vocalist. Some musicians make it big by simply playing instrumentals, but the ones that do are phenomenal musicians. It takes nearly super human technical ability to become famous from technical skill alone, but combine less technical ability with solid vocal melodies and you are much closer to making it than someone that simply plays noise.

How to Demand a Paycheck

The Rule of Number One.

The first thing that we all must learn when playing music together is that there is only one "Number One" in any band. The only interest that "Number One" has is staying number one.

All other band members are hired for one purpose. That is to make number one sound the very best he/she possibly can. Nobody can take away from number one and expect to stay with the group. Many musicians have ego problems and like to show off just what they know or what they can do. When playing as a band and you distract the audience from number one your job may be short-lived. The only time that number one is not number one is when he takes a break in the vocals and allows one of the musicians to play the turnaround or the break itself in the song. When an instrument takes a break, it becomes number one which is only temporary and then it reverts back to the singer himself. Regardless of how good you are as a musician, you must realize that you will always be number two in any band where there is a singer. Remember the first part of this book the singer is always number one and your job is to accompany him in order to make him sound the best possible.

When the instrument that takes the break becomes number one, the job of the other musicians is to support him and make him sound the very best that they possibly can. That means that you cannot play louder than him, you cannot do things to distract the audience from him, because if you do it breaks that ring that bans a group together. Sometimes it takes five people playing together for years before they ever get the ideas of what it takes to actually get the sound that they are after. One reason for this is many musicians either do not want to hear what needs to be done to "fix" their music, or people are afraid of giving them the constructive criticism they need. Do not be afraid of giving your opinion on what needs to be done, but if you do, do so in a manner that is subtle. One way of doing this is by making them believe it was their idea. Few people like being told their music is slightly off, and even fewer actually know where their problem is. Vision a band in a recording studio. Whose job is it to play the instruments? Now whose job is it to make all of the music fit together in perfect balance? It's the engineer's job of course.

I have always enjoyed teaching groups to actually become a band rather than individuals. It's amazing when a group of five or more will come to you and ask for help. One of the things that you learn, your voice is an instrument. The more you practice using your voice the better you will become. 10 hours on a guitar will not give you the satisfaction that you would get using your voice 10 hours. We have been using our voices as musical instruments since the day we were born. We hum as children, sing in church, and speak all day long. In theory it should be easier to train your voice for music than to learn any stringed instrument. The key factor is the amount of time spent training. For me it is nothing to sit and play banjo for two hours, and this is probably true for most musicians. Dedicate your instrument playing time to vocal playing time. While you are playing a melody slow it down and hum to it. Each note practiced will build to a bigger picture of your musical talent.

How to Demand a Paycheck

The thing I enjoyed most while teaching is the harmonizing of the vocal parts. The lead singer will always be number one. Now you have other voice ranges tenor, baritone, and bass. Regardless of what key that the lead singer is singing in, in order to harmonize with this person you must be able to get your voice in different octaves to sing tenor, baritone or bass. Singing harmony means that you not only have to sing in the key that the lead singer is in but you also must be able to get over him or under him. Your vocal range will be determined by your breathing. This does not sound right to you. Once you begin practicing using your voice as an instrument, you have the right timing to come in with the music you will notice that your breathing will help you provide the right timing. Then you will understand what I'm saying about how important it is to use your breathing and practice your breathing when singing. To sing bass it takes more wind capacity to sing the low notes than it does to sing tenor or lead. You must not only learn how to sing in different keys, but you must learn how to breathe.

How to Demand a Paycheck

So many of the things that you want to practice when playing and singing together are real simple, but if you never really think of what you want to do to make your group sound as one, you never stop to think to get each one's opinion, what it sounds like, what would make it sound better.

As an individual each one of us knows something that the other doesn't. Each one of us has been trained in a different field. You may know more about a guitar, I may know more about a banjo. The other person in the band with you may specialize in math, biology, or farming. The things that each one of us learned in life will attribute our knowledge that we know something that maybe somebody else doesn't know. If we applied this to the group and when we ask for each one's opinion as to what would make us sound better, each one will have their contribution. By listening to each other, trying different things, you can become a band.

How to Demand a Paycheck

As a singer, we must try to decide who has the best singing voice, the clarity of the words that they are singing and vocal range that they have and are able to use. As a singer the most sought after things that you can strive for is clarity of the words that you pronounce because if your audience cannot understand some of the words you sing, you have wasted your time. Sometimes the lead singer may be able to do a better job singing harmony than he does the lead on certain songs. This is why they call it practice. Never decide just because you know a song that you have to be the one that sings the lead on it.

One of the most useful tools to help you with your practice sessions is a recorder. The easiest thing to do is to work out a song, record it and then listen back. If you listen to this back as a group you will be able to sort out the things that you liked about it or the things that you dislike about it. The things that you liked most about it you work the hardest on and try to improve those. The things that you don't like, change those to something that you do like better. There's nothing that says a song has to be done exactly like the original person that recorded it. The good Lord gave us all different voices. By having different voices we also have different abilities as part of the keys and the way that we can sing or play.

Never be afraid to say to yourself I don't think my playing or singing is contributing to this group. Maybe I should try a different instrument or try different vocal ranges. Just because you bring five persons together that can play and sing individually it's not going to make a group. Sometimes no matter how much you practice the sounds that you're striving to develop may never come about. If you look at the other groups that are top bluegrass groups in their field, you will see that they change musicians and singers sometimes more often than their socks. Back to the beginning as to what we started writing this book for, constructive criticism can cause your feelings to be hurt or make you think who do they think they are telling me that I have a problem whether it be singing, or playing. It could be the question you must ask yourself; what am I contributing to this group?

How to Demand a Paycheck

If you don't like the answer that you can tell yourself, you must work on improving your contribution. The reasons for writing this small book are to help musicians and singers, that they might understand themselves better as to their job in a band.

Another of the more important things that we must learn in order to become a stage group, is that the closer we can get our heads together when singing harmony, the easier that it is to blend our voices with each other. Sometimes we may have to change our standing positions to become closer and more understanding of the harmonies that we are doing and the abilities to take a break with the instruments when called upon.

If you were old enough to remember, or have seen a film of groups on stage, and try to find Lester Flat, Bill Monroe, Jim and Jesse McReynolds and so many other top bluegrass musicians and singers and watched their performance, a lot of times, they would use only one microphone and number one which would be the lead singer or when he take a break and the vocals the other musician that would pick the lead would become number one, temporarily would stand in different positions in order to use that one microphone. That type of performance is what makes bluegrass music famous. Go back and try to find some of the old film or video. The more you can duplicate the type of performances that the professionals did 50 years ago, the more you will stand out as better musicians and singers as a group.

One of the most interesting things that I have found over the years, the groups today do not separate themselves from their audience. The groups of yesteryear, when they stepped on stage, they did not look like anyone else in the audience. A lot of times, there would be better singers and musicians sitting in the audience than there were on stage. The main difference between the persons in the audience and the persons on stage was that the persons in the audience did not have the drive or the ambition to become a star. One of the main differences between the musician and the audience and the musicians on stage is the level of work that each one is willing to do. The persons on stage usually consider their music as their life's work. The persons in the audience usually work at jobs that have a steady paycheck but play music for the fun of it. The persons in the audience usually have a desire to own more material things other than an instrument and being able to sing.

Some of the groups that I run into today have members that have played together for possibly 20 years. But in that same 20 year span, have never sat down and talked about their career, where it was going or what they expected from it. They never discuss the clothes that they wear, the hats they wear, or their personal appearance. They will talk as to why they don't get hired to play the paying jobs. The discussion of their stage appearance never comes up. They never see themselves through the eye of a camera. Do we look our best in the eye of the audience? Do we look at ourselves through our eyes and ears to determine why our audience should pay to see us or are we just the average bunch of guys that want to get on stage for a short time?

How to Demand a Paycheck

Back in the late 70s, the top bluegrass musicians or country singers that walked among their audience talking with them, sitting down to play music or just walking among them. They always dressed nice, usually in their stage clothes which automatically separated them from their audience. Most always when these musicians were spoken to, they were referred to as Mr. or Mrs. Very seldom by their first names. This was a show of respect for the musician or singer which set them apart from their audience. This is why the audience is willing to pay to see these people and listen to them.

The next statements printed here are my own opinions about each musician as to how I think they need to dress when expecting a paycheck. The first thing; shower, shave, never wear tennis shoes, shine your shoes or boots, wear dress pants and matching shirts that fit. Never wear clothes that are wrinkled or look slept in. Remember, you are going for a paycheck. If your hair is long enough to comb, make sure you have a comb in your pocket. Always use cologne, aftershave, and deodorant. Remember what your gold is; a paycheck.

If I wanted a date with the most beautiful woman you had ever seen, how would you present yourself as being worthy to ask her for a date? Would she consider going out with you the way you look now or the way you can look? The first impression that I wish to place upon her mind, I hope will be the best. I think men and women should read the statements; I want to look my very best when I'm with you or whether I'm going on stage. Each of us has to ask ourselves when we see others that are attractive, what can I do to make myself more attractive? Sometimes, all we have to do is look in a mirror. Our audience is the world we live in and remember how they see us will be what our rewards are based upon.

The instruments that we play on stage or in our personal lives will never make music for us without us playing them. The name brands regardless of who else owns one or plays one will never sound the same as when you play. You have to be satisfied with your own instrument. Three things you must like about your instrument; the looks are one of the most important, the sound is the next, and the playability which can be altered by any person that understands how to set an instrument up correctly. If you like those three things, you got a bargain regardless of how much you paid for. The price you pay for your instrument only gives you bragging rights as to the value. The most expensive instruments in the world can never have a guarantee that says it is going to be the best sounding, the best playing, or the most beautiful instrument you could purchase for your money. All of these things can only be judged by the person that owns this instrument.

After being in the music business for 35 years, one of the things that I have discovered about buying instruments; never buy one that you can't put your hands on and play because the name on that instrument is not what makes music, it's you yourself.

How to Demand a Paycheck

The most important thing that I have learned about handcrafted instruments; the Lord never made two trees alike. Consider this statement that there's no two instruments alike, even though they may have been built by the same person on the same design. The sound is also going to be different as will the playability. Choose the instrument that you are going to play and sing with as to the playability of your skills and a sound that will match your voice when singing.

If you need help choosing an instrument that will meet your needs, stop in at Tennessee Sounds, 1001 N. Eastman Rd., Greenacres Plaza, Kingsport, TN 37664. Or go to TennesseeSounds.com.

If you would like some personal help putting your group together and getting the best sounds that you possibly can you can call me at Tennessee sounds Victor Jenkins. Like I had stated I have over 30 years of experience teaching but not only individual lessons for group lessons and groups themselves to actually become better musicians and better singers. I charge by the hour and groups that wish to become a band by the number of people in the group. I no longer teach private lessons for individuals. Over many years of teaching today's students think they should be able to play within 30 days regardless of what their skill levels are. If you are a teacher yourself you should understand how frustrating this is to spend extra time with students and then they decide they're not going to be able to do it. The teachers in public schools I commend them that they can stay in classes tried to teach with students that aren't really interested in learning. So many students wish to play an instrument to please their parents or their friends.

One lesson in life; anything that you decide to do in life and wish to do it well make it a priority because if it's not that important to you it's definitely not as important to someone else. I have turned down many students over the last 30 years that have come in stating they would like to take lessons because they think they want to learn to play. If you think you want to learn to play and it's not a priority that you are definitely going to do, why should it be a priority for someone else?

One of my experiences; a dad and his son came into my store in Michigan and the dad told me that he would like to get a guitar for his son to learn to play. I asked him if he played guitar. His answer was I have one but mostly it sits in the corner. My next question; have you asked your son if he would like to learn to play a guitar? Another little part of my story, I also owned a motorcycle dealership in Michigan and the music store. The son was out looking at all the motorcycles when I asked his dad where was he. I called the kid into the music department and asked him if he wanted to learn to play guitar. His answer instantly was no. His dad looked at me right funny looking and I told him, you have already taught him that if you own a guitar you don't have to play it, let it sit in the corner. I lost the sale of a guitar by being honest with the boys dad and the boy and I hope it was a lesson he never forgets.

How to Demand a Paycheck

This is another little story that might help with the group you're trying to form. Being honest with each other when forming a band that you hope will carry you through music enjoyment for years is a necessity.

I was just talking to Cody Jennings of 100.7 radio out of Bristol. Cody is the announcer for the country and bluegrass number one music station in this part of the country. We were talking about this book I'm writing and my goals as far as getting this out to the people that are interested in making a band instead of five individuals. I will be letting Cody read this book before we put it to the Internet because his opinions to me are very useful. By him being in the music industry, he sometimes works with new groups and professional groups. He also sees the flaws in the singing and playing that each group runs into.

This book to be heard or read and studied; Constructive criticism can come in many forms. It can be from books written on this subject that has come from professional musicians, people that make a living playing music and singing, or it can be from a friend or possibly someone you are actually playing with. The most easily understood lessons are from print, not what someone else says to you.

Now we can get into the type of instruments that you choose to use in your playing and singing. The first lesson; never choose an instrument that someone else to choses tells you is the very best. Their choice may not be what suits you. As a singer and a musician, if you are choosing a guitar, let someone else help you choose the sound that most suit your voice. Most guitars have either two types of sound. One is more bass and midrange; the other will have midrange and treble. Look for a guitar that has a balanced type of sound from the bass through the treble. There are thousands of guitars available but if you choose a guitar with the balanced type of sound check out Taylor. Taylor guitars are now the number one sold acoustic guitar in the United States. The main reason for this is not only the quality but they build over 140 models to suit any musician and any type of music that you wish to play. Their total line of guitars, from the least expensive, through their strictly top-of-the-line are based on a balanced type of sound. One guitar may have a deeper tone with less sustain, another may have a more ringing brighter sound with more sustain. Guitars with more sustain and a smaller body, are more suited for fingerpicking styles.

For bluegrass type of playing and singing, the musician likes a guitar with a deeper tone, a balanced type of sound with an overall sound that works for playing rhythm or picking lead.

By talking to other musicians that are in the music field and listening to their opinions of what it takes to be a professional bluegrass musician or singer, are some of the things that I put in for bluegrass musicians, will choose a guitar with Rosewood sides and back. They like a guitar with the dreadnought style body. They choose the dreadnought style body because they see others playing that same type of guitar. Not always the best. Again from the first part of this book; I have been in the music business over 35 years. The guitar that I play is a Taylor 814 that I had custom built by

How to Demand a Paycheck

Taylor for myself. I have small hands. The neck on my guitar has a width of 1 11/16 rather than an inch and three-quarter. I did not have the cutaway done on my guitar but I did have the three piece back in matching Rosewood done on the back, the binding on my guitar is all flame Maple, and I also had the expression system pickup put in my guitar just in case I plug up to an amp or PA system. In 35 years of being in the music business, I have had choices of thousands of guitars. This Taylor Guitar beats anything that I have ever owned for me.

For every customer that comes into my store, if he/she is a guitar player I will let them play my guitar just to get their opinion. We have all types of guitars in stock that they may possibly own. We invite everyone to bring their personal guitar in to compare it to the guitars of we have in stock. Before you ever choose an instrument for yourself, the best idea of helping you to choose one for yourself is to compare what your friend thinks is the best to the other guitars of your choice. You make the decision, not your friends.

How to Demand a Paycheck

Again, a name brand may not be the instrument that you choose. Again, your first consideration when looking at an instrument is, does it look good? The next thing, does it sound good. Can the playability be changed to suit my needs? When you find an instrument with these three qualities, you bought a bargain. There are thousands of used instruments but the person that sold that instrument may have decided that it was not the best instrument for him. Most people looking for their first instrument, their choice is made by price rather than the three above qualities that you should look for. These three qualities does not mean the most expensive or the best deal. Your choice should be an instrument that will suit your needs for the money you have. If this instrument has the three above qualities; you bought a bargain. If you look at the instrument that you wish to buy as an investment for life; make your choice wisely. Do not, again, do not let your friend influence you as to what your needs are.

The choices that we make can change our lives forever. The life we live is determined by the choices we make. We have two types of decisions that we must make in life. One is good decisions, the other is bad decisions.

Maybe I should get off the soapbox and make a few more decisions as to how to help you become the band that you would love to be in. Try to make decisions about your group that will help each one in the group, whether it be singer or musician. Your audience will judge you by your first appearance. Your language is determined by what you wish to say and the intelligence you display. Again first appearance is everything. Next, the clothing that you wear, your personal appearance will all be judged before you open your mouth to sing or to play. You should never tell a joke using profanity, never cut down one of the band members just for a laugh, and always be respectful to your audience as though it was your mother, proud of her son or daughter playing for her.

The comments that I have made in the above paragraph will help you to rise on the ladder of success when you ask for a paycheck. My goal is to help you make decisions that will not only help you in the music field, but will help you in your personal life as well. Most of the decisions we make in life determines how much we respect ourselves.

Our ambitions are limited as to what we want in life. If it's just a paycheck, get a job at a filling station or anything else. If you wish a paycheck with the recognition of the things that you have accomplished, in life, your ambition is determined by the number of times you climb up, fall down, and climb up again.

I would like to thank each and every one of you that has purchased this book with my hope, that it will help you in your life, to become a better musician, a better singer, a band of one, with a type of sound that will take you to the top. The next thing that I hope for you, would be to help you become the person you wish to be. I had thought seriously about this book before I wrote it and hope to be able to condense it down so that it would be easily read and understood so that you could use it yourself to improve your position in a group.

Victor Jenkins

How to Demand a Paycheck

Tennessee Sounds
1001 N. Eastman Rd. Suite C,
Greenacres Shopping plaza
Kingsport, Tennessee-37664
1-423-245-4005,
toll-free 1-855-238-9218.

If you wish to call about this article that I have written, please feel free. I will try to answer your questions concerning any subject of this book. Our website is TennesseeSounds.com. If you call with your e-mail address, we send out newsletters once a week pertaining to new products, things we're doing, and other suggestions that may help you with what you're doing. Again, thank you. Vic

About the Author

Vic Jenkins was born in Carswell Hollow, West Virginia during the cold winter of 1941. He is a man of many talents and experiences. He worked in the coal mines, drove a taxi, broke and trained horses, done machinist work, started several businesses over the years, and got in a little trouble along the way. He is a military veteran, a motorcycle rider, and a fine banjo picker. But above all he is a man that wants to help people that are willing to help themselves. Currently he is the owner of Tennessee Sounds, a musical instrument store located in Kingsport. There he is doing incredible things that most old men have never imagined; he has published DVD's, a book, and many more to come over the next 1000 years!

www.ingramcontent.com/pod-product-compliance
Lightning Source LLC
Chambersburg PA
CBHW031336040426
42443CB00005B/370